CEO at 20: A Little Book for Big Dreams

by Ben Gothard

CEO & Founder of Gothard Enterprises LLC

Ben Gothard

104 Geneva St.

Metairie, LA 70005

For more information, contact me at
bgothard@gothardenterprises.com .

ISBN: 0997812400

ACKNOWLEDGMENTS

To my father,
Dad, you have always been my biggest role model. I can always count on your wisdom, strength and love, and I strive to make you proud every day. I wish I could put in words how thankful I am for you. This book would not have been possible without you. I love you.

To my mother,
Mom, you are kindest, most gracious and sweetest person that I know. You have always shown me unconditional love, taken care of me, and made me a better person. I owe everything that I am to you, and cannot even begin to say thank you enough. I love you.

To my editors,
Mrs. Johnson and Aunt Shayna, you two are brilliant, incredibly talented individuals. Thank you so much for helping me accomplish my dream of writing this book. I am forever grateful.

To you,
Thank you for choosing to read my very first book. It took me a year to write, and I have grown tremendously in the process. I hope to add something positive to your life.

CEO AT 20: A LITTLE BOOK FOR BIG DREAMS

Do you have a dream but don't know how to make it a reality? If so, you're not alone. Many people have dreams, the diversity and scope of which are limitless. Some dream of climbing Mt. Everest, starting a school, getting a degree, or finding that special someone with whom to share a lifetime. While many people have dreams, most never achieve them. There are plenty of reasons why those dreams remain unfulfilled, but one is particularly stifling. Many people view their dreams passively, as something to wish for which will never be attained. In this book, I hope to provide some motivation and practical advice about how to turn your dreams into reality.

IT'S NEVER TOO EARLY TO START!

Our time on Earth is finite, but accomplishing a dream takes time. Think about your typical day. How much of it is spent doing things you are passionate about? We all get bogged down by life's everyday demands. Unfortunately, many never make the time to chase their dreams. Whether or not you use your time wisely is up to you, because only you control when, if ever, you start the process of pursuing a specific dream. It is a decision you must make, and the earlier the better. Time will pass; nothing can change that. The only thing you can control is what you accomplish in the time you are given. The sooner you start your journey, the more time you have to accomplish your goals. Plus, working on the process when you are young has its advantages. Youth has energy, innovation, and passion to get things done. When you are young - especially if you are a student - people may be more willing to share their time and advice with you out of goodwill.

There is no reason not to start pursuing your dreams at an early age. Shortly after turning 20 years old, I had two conversations that changed my life forever. The first was with my roommate, an aspiring film director and entrepreneur. At the beginning of our sophomore year at Louisiana State University, my roommate and I had a conversation about his t-shirt business. He needed help marketing and I was looking for something to put on my resume. At around the same time, my father, a New Orleans attorney, mentioned that he was looking for someone to help market his law firm on social media. I told them both that I was interested, but wanted them to pay my soon-to-be company instead of me. I took the first major step in chasing my own dreams by starting a social media marketing company; Gothard Enterprises LLC was legally formed on December 19, 2014. I was officially a C.E.O. at 20. Was I ready to tackle the challenges of running a business and being a full time college student at such an early age? The only way to find out was to try, and I wasn't going to let anything, especially my age, stop me.

IT'S NEVER TOO LATE TO START!

As you get older, you will likely have more responsibility. Marriage, children, and career may significantly limit the time available to devote to accomplishing your dreams. Not only is there a shortage of time, but many people don't want to start a new and intimidating journey. They don't want to take the risk, because they fear failure, change, and/or the weight of their responsibilities. Many people choose to stay in a set routine – their comfort zone - where they know exactly what is going to happen. No matter your age, if you don't break out of a self-created mold, you will never accomplish anything new. Fear of failure will halt any possibility of success and accomplishment. Your actions, not your age, define what you can do. If you have the desire to accomplish something, you must act. There is precisely one right time to start chasing your dreams – now! My father often says, "nobody ever reached the finish line without first crossing the starting line" – both simple and profoundly accurate. I challenge you to take that first step, but its up to you to challenge yourself and go.

Colonel Harland David Sanders didn't let his age stop him from pursuing his dreams. Born in 1890, Colonel Sanders held odd jobs until around age 40 when he started working on a chicken recipe. It wasn't until he was 62, however, that he opened the first Kentucky Fried Chicken (KFC) franchise. In the meantime, he lived in his car, relied on governmental entitlement programs, and struggled to convince potential franchise owners to buy and use his recipe. Despite constant rejection, he persevered, and earned his place in history as the founder of one of the first fast food chains to expand internationally. Colonel Sanders is one of many examples of those whose ambition and efforts were actualized at a later age, and still achieved great success and fulfillment.

While youth has its inherent advantages to achieving success, so does maturity and experience. Over time, many accumulate knowledge through education and experiences and develop discipline and a responsible work ethic. This is the path to maturity and wisdom. These are invaluable assets that an older person may possess, and which may enhance the possibility of success in your endeavors. Age is not your enemy and definitely not an excuse.

DEVELOP A PLAN!

At this point you might be thinking, "I get it! I want to start! I'm ready to start! But how?" It would be nice to get a letter in your in-box telling you exactly what to do, but that's not likely to happen. You start by making a plan. If you were going to take a road trip, you wouldn't walk out of the house empty-handed and start driving unless you didn't care where you ended up, i.e. had no goal. If, on the other hand, you had a destination, then you would develop a plan, pack your bags with appropriate clothing and supplies, fill up the car with gas, and map out the journey. Then, you would execute the plan. Chasing your dreams is no different because chasing your dreams is a journey – possibly the most rewarding journey of your life.

Let's explore the concept of developing a plan in more detail through a hypothetical hike in the forest. Before you start, you have to figure out the big details. Where you would like to hike? What route do you want to take? When do you want to go? What would you like to see on your hike? In other words, you identify a goal. You could hike to an amazing waterfall, investigate abandoned ruins, discover a new trail, or simply have a day of exercise. Without this crucial step – identifying your goal - you will likely wind up walking aimlessly with no food, water, or supplies. You might see an animal or happen across a stream if you are lucky, but most likely you will just be walking in the woods. On the other hand, you could plan out your hike properly with a goal in mind. With a plan, you can pack the right clothing, bring the appropriate amounts of food and water, and find an accurate map. These are your tools. You can reach your intended destination because you are prepared and have a plan of action. The truth is that we have no control over nature, and probably less control over ourselves than we would like to admit. There are any number of unlikely and unforeseeable obstacles that may ultimately prevent you from attaining your goals. A plan helps you control the things you can, prepare for the things you cannot control, and maximize the probability of success.

The same goes for your life. If you plan it out properly, you give yourself the best odds to succeed. Do you want to own your own business? Start by writing a business plan! Do you dream of being a professional athlete? Start by developing a workout and nutrition plan! Do you aspire to raise a family in the suburbs and live a quiet, happy life? Start by mapping out your ideal scenario with your significant other! When you plan, you dramatically increase your chances of accomplishing your goals by actively preparing for the future. You are choosing your own path. You are designing the trail map to your future.

I learned the importance of planning in building my company. My initial goal was for Gothard Enterprises to be a successful social media marketing firm, but without a clear idea of how that might happen. The work, however, was clear - help clients build a community around their brand through different social media platforms (Facebook, Twitter, Instagram, etc.) by identifying a target market, acquiring potential customers, and helping them manage the community. I quickly realized the need for a plan. I created a business plan for my company, detailing what I wanted to accomplish and how I was going to get there. Planning out the work created a clear focus and organized vision, which inspired and motivated my whole company. Plans lead to results, and results lead to success. Whatever the goal, you will benefit from forethought and planning.

WHAT SHOULD MY DREAM BE?

A dream can be anything. However, I would suggest finding something that is meaningful to you. Our time is finite, so you should think through what you believe your dream to be, and what your life will be like if you accomplish it. If you are struggling to identify what your dream could be, try thinking about how you would answer these questions: What is really important to me? What am I the best at? What do I spend my leisure time doing? It is normal to struggle when trying to answer these questions. Some people know exactly what they want to do when they "grow up." The rest of us develop interests over time. Don't panic if you have no burning passions yet. Rather, pay closer attention to yourself. Notice what makes you feel good about yourself. When you look inside for insight, you might be pleasantly surprised at what you discover.

Once you identify an area of interest, the only limitations are those you impose on yourself. What you accomplish is directly correlated to the goals you set. The more ambitious a goal, the better. Do you think many people believed Walt Disney was rational, logical, or realistic when he articulated his dream of a Land of Disney? What do you think his odds of success were at the beginning? Walt Disney had a dream, made a plan, and dedicated his life to seeing it through. It took him a lifetime, but he built an empire that continues to flourish and grow, as does his legacy, well after his death. Today, the Disney Empire is a multi-billion dollar international conglomerate consisting of five vacation resorts, eleven theme parks, two water parks, thirty-nine hotels, eight motion picture studios, six record labels, eleven cable television networks, and a local television network as of 2015. According to their 2013 annual report, the company had yearly revenues of over $45 billion with approximately 175,000 employees. Walt Disney was a wildly ambitious dreamer and a remarkably focused planner.

PASSION

Before you start your journey, you can learn a lot by studying common problems faced by others who successfully, and unsuccessfully, chased their dreams. Arguably the most prominent problem is a lack of sincere interest, or passion. Jason Nazar, Founder & C.E.O of Docstoc, described it this way: "If you don't have a why, you will let the what and how get in your way and be your excuse for not doing something." In other words, if you do not have a sincere interest in the goal, you will likely be defeated by the effort and decisions necessary to reach the goal. Without passion, you will be inclined to stop dead in your tracks at the first sign of trouble, give up, and go home. Invariably, there will be trouble. On your journey, you can expect to encounter financial setbacks, emotional discomfort, stress, and repeated failure. When the going gets tough, and you feel that you can't make it, your passion will give you the energy to persevere.

The things in life that are the most rewarding and special are often the most difficult to accomplish. If something is easy to do, then it isn't very special because anyone is able to do it. Binge watching Netflix's latest series is definitely fun, but not an impressive accomplishment and probably not as satisfying as climbing Mt. Everest. If you want to accomplish something difficult, attach that goal to your identity, harness your passion, and give it absolutely everything you have. Passion is what keeps you going despite difficulty and setbacks. You have to find your passion, your "why." Only then can you persevere on your journey and accomplish the incredible things you are capable of doing.

I look for passion in my employees - passion for learning, growing, teamwork, and success. Specifically, I look for dedication to the vision of the future of Gothard Enterprises. With passion comes the attention to detail, desire for improvement, and unrelenting fortitude necessary to start a company from scratch and succeed. When a team is passionate about a common goal, the energy is palpable and powerful. Finding, recruiting, and training every single person in my company was a difficult process. I spoke with a number of very smart and capable men and women, but not every applicant was a good fit for the company. I made mistakes and had to fire several individuals who just didn't fit. Though difficult, it was a necessary thing to do in order to put together a team with a common passion and a common goal. My passion for the business has helped me make difficult decisions, motivate the rest of the team, and persevere despite failure. Passion gets you through hard times. Passion will lead to success, regardless of the effort and sacrifice required along the way.

WORK ETHIC

Intelligence, luck, timing, and a tremendous amount of work are all necessary in accomplishing your goals. American entrepreneur and NBA Maverick's owner Mark Cuban insists, "Effort is the one thing you can control in your life." Cuban, along with most successful people, realized that one of the few variables in life that you have complete control over is how hard you work. Everyone has unique strengths and weaknesses. There are people who are smarter and stronger than you, just as you possess natural gifts that others don't. You are trying to reach your goals with your skill set. That's life. You are not in a competition with anyone, not even yourself. You are on a journey to maximize your potential and achieve your goals. It isn't worth your time or energy to worry about what other people are or are not doing. That will only distract you from what your focus should be – your own path.

At Gothard Enterprises, we know our work ethic is a way to distinguish ourselves from the competition. We do work in a timely manner. We set benchmarks and meet every week to check progress. Clients have responded positively to our corporate personality. We need a competitive advantage to secure clients. That advantage is work ethic. Established businessmen and women appreciate our willingness to work as hard as need be to do an excellent job for them. Through our work ethic, we establish credibility and develop expertise. On any worthwhile journey, you have to be willing to try hard. When, not if, you struggle and fail, you need to get back up and try harder. If you don't reach a particular goal having given your best effort, learn from it and succeed next time.

MINDSET

You need conviction and confidence to reach your goals. If you don't believe that you are destined for greatness, then you aren't. If you don't aim for the stars, you will always shoot the sand. According to research, a positive mindset is proven to lead to more success than a negative one.

Dr. Carol Dweck, author and professor of psychology at Stanford University, breaks down the human mindset into two categories – fixed and growth - and applies them to different aspects of life, including challenges, obstacles, effort, criticism, and the success of others. The fixed mindset comes from the belief that intelligence is static. This belief leads to a desire to look smart. People with this mindset have a tendency to run away from challenges, give up easily when faced with obstacles, regard effort as a waste of time, and ignore negative criticism. They feel insecure and threatened by the success of others. People with this mindset typically plateau early in their lives and never reach their full potential, confirming and reinforcing a deterministic view of the world.

The growth mindset, on the other hand, is based on the belief that intelligence can be developed, which leads to a desire to learn. In other words, an interest in being smart rather than appearing to be smart. With this mindset, there is a tendency to face challenges head on, persevere despite failure, view effort as necessary to mastery, learn from criticism, and become motivated by the success of others. A growth mindset is critical to accomplishing your dreams because it can lead to extremely high levels of achievement and a much greater sense of free will. Every successful journey involves learning and personal growth. If the door to your mind is fixed, and not open to criticism, creativity, and learning from others, your journey may be quite rough. A growth mindset helps to turn setbacks into learning opportunities. Hardships become challenges that make you stronger, and failure becomes great motivation to succeed.

The things we achieve in life are directly correlated to the goals we set. While it might be common sense, it doesn't make those goals any easier. A proper mindset might. Olympian Michael Phelps had an insatiable hunger for victory, coupled with the mindset of a winner. His growth mindset connected his natural physical attributes and his extraordinary work ethic. Throughout his career, Phelps honed his natural abilities, persevered during tough times, and was always open to learn. Phelps won 23 Olympic gold medals, a feat never done before, undisputedly making him the most successful Olympian in history. That he has a growth mindset is no coincidence. Rather, it's one critical component to his success.

Does this mean you will accomplish everything that you set your mind to? Though a growth mindset does not guarantee success on your journey, a fixed mindset just about guarantees failure. If you are taking a road trip and declare you cannot go any farther than 100 miles, you will almost surely stop when you reach that interval. You are establishing a fixed cap, a limit. A fixed mindset will convince every part of your being that you are limited, and it becomes self-fulfilling. If, on the other hand, you decide to drive as far as you can, you may well travel farther than 100 miles. You may still get fatigued before reaching your final destination, but at least you didn't put a pre-determined limit on yourself; you allowed yourself to remain open and adaptable. If you don't have the conviction that your dreams will become reality, they probably will not. If you don't have an open, positive mindset, you will not believe in yourself, and no one else will either.

A great way to facilitate your journey is to objectively evaluate your mindset. Are you open to change? Are you eager and willing to grow? Or do you believe that you have all of the answers right now, that no one has anything of value to teach? I challenge you to categorize your own mindset, find some areas that can be improved, and start thinking big.

FINANCE

Now that you are motivated and have a plan, let's discuss some tools that could be useful on your journey. If your dream is business oriented or large in scale, you will more than likely need to acquire capital. Financing can be complicated, particularly if you are young and have a limited ability to get a traditional bank loan or line of credit. Fortunately, there are new, nontraditional ways to raise significant amounts of money at little cost to you. Kickstarter, GoFundMe and Prosper are all considered to be peer-to-peer (P2P) crowd funding mechanisms, and may help you on your journey.

The first tool to consider is Kickstarter. This site's goal is to "help artists, musicians, filmmakers, designers, and other creators find the resources and support they need to make their ideas a reality." People from around the world post their current "projects." After setting a financial goal needed to finish the project, people from around the world can pledge money to help. The beauty of Kickstarter is there are no traditional financial returns for donating to a certain project. Instead, the person who posted the project offers rewards, such as an autographed shirt, a mention in a book, a backstage pass, etc. Fortunately for the investor, if the entire stated goal is not reached by the designated time limit, the project does not get funded at all and the money is returned. There are few limitations on Kickstarter, and most projects are eligible for funding.

An alternative to Kickstarter is GoFundMe. This website is similar to Kickstarter in that each individual donates a small portion to the overall goal. There are three types of campaigns: personal, charity, and all-or-nothing (most similar to Kickstarter). Unlike Kickstarter, GoFundMe does not offer rewards for donations. Instead, the site allows you to update all of your backers with the latest news on your project in order to stimulate continued interest in your goal and keep everyone in the loop. The upside to GoFundMe is that there are no deadlines or goal requirements. You keep every donation you receive, and there are no penalties for missing your goal. GoFundMe is a better option for those with ambitious monetary goals because you can keep trying until you reach it. However, GoFundMe is unfavorable for the investor, since the project is funded regardless of whether or not the entire stated goal is reached by the designated time limit. Like Kickstarter, there are few restrictions, so it is up to you to decide which platform is most appropriate.

A third alternative is Prosper. Unlike Kickstarter and GoFundMe, Prosper uses a financially driven model, classified as peer-to-peer (P2P) lending. Those needing a loan apply on the website, and, pending approval, can open up that loan to the public. The public has the opportunity to participate in the loan, where individuals can invest as little as $25 or as large as the entire loan. For the borrower, this can mean significantly lower rates and fees than a traditional loan. The investor, on the other hand, has the ability to participate in many loans and build a portfolio with hopefully better returns than traditional investing.

Ideally, you will not need to borrow a great deal at the beginning of your journey. Many new businesses fail because they unrealistically evaluate their business model. They incur debt that they are ultimately unable to repay. If you must seek financing on the way to your dream, make sure you are knowledgeable, or get the advice of someone who is, about your chosen platform and business model.

GUIDANCE

Another crucial tool to advance your journey is guidance in the form of a mentor. Mentoring is an age-old concept, tracing back to ancient Greece as a technique to "impart to young men [and women] important social, spiritual, and personal values" (Metros and Yang). Young men and women would seek out experienced craftsmen in order to learn a specific skill, such as blacksmithing, baking, or shoemaking. The craftsmen would take on an apprentice, teach the professional craft, and pass down wisdom and insight gained from experience. In modern times, we look to higher education as an alternative to apprenticeship. This can be unfortunate in many respects, as there are many things that can only be learned from real world experience. While formal education is a wonderful source of knowledge and information, one on one attention from a skilled, experienced mentor provides access to wisdom that can only be gained through real world experience.

Accomplished, experienced mentors don't just appear – you have to actively seek them out. Ideally, you want to find someone who has already done what you are trying to do, and is willing to answer your questions and pass on their knowledge. You should slowly, respectfully, and carefully attempt to get to know a potential mentor, with opportunity for them to get to know you too.

It is important to identify which mentoring style would be best for you. According to research at the Ohio State University, there are seven distinct types of mentors. The first is the wise leader, a person who has reached the top of their field and is willing to pass on their knowledge to others. These mentors are typically confident, natural leaders who have thrived in their field for a long period of time. For example, the owner or a top executive of a company may have the knowledge and experience you seek. Wise leaders are usually prominent in their communities and stretched for time; such a person will not be willing to part with their valuable time or expertise unless they see serious potential in you as a mentee.

The second mentoring style is the life coach: professional mentors who evaluate performance, offer self-improvement advice, identify professional opportunities, and help their clients set and achieve both personal and professional goals. Coaching relationships are typically not long-term, but designed to identify and accomplish a specific set of meaningful objectives. This makes life coaches very valuable. A primary distinction between life coaches and other mentor types is the price; life coaches are professionals who expect to be paid, and good ones are expensive! Fortunately, many life coaches now work on-line, and the influx in supply may drive the price down. If affordable to you, a good life coach properly suited to you in experience and temperament can be an incredible resource to you on your journey.

The teacher is the third type of mentor. They are educators who facilitate the growth of professional skills by "imparting knowledge, debating ideas, or recommending resources" (Metros and Yang). A teaching mentor relationship can be as formal as an independent study or as casual as chatting during office hours. If you are a student, speak with local professors in your field of interest. You want to look for a teacher with the skills, knowledge, and experience that can aid you on your journey and will give you the time and attention that you need. The difference between a professor in a classroom setting and a teaching mentor is the personal relationship you would cultivate outside of the formal classroom setting.

The fourth type of mentor is the peer mentor. This is typically an informal relationship in which colleagues or friends work together in a common field or endeavor. You can assist each other in networking, problem solving, and positive encouragement, among other things. In a professional setting, peers often complement each other's strengths and weaknesses, creating a partnership that is stronger than the sum of its separate parts. Trustworthy, accountable peers can be an incredible resource on your journey. They can challenge you to be your best and serve as valuable allies. An effective partnership involves sharing responsibility and watching out for one another, both of which can lead to empowerment and further progression on your journey. Peers who understand your particular challenges may also be uniquely positioned for encouragement during tough times.

The fifth mentoring style is the confidante. These people are not so much mentors as individuals to bounce ideas off of and talk things over with. On every meaningful journey there will be setbacks, and yours will be no different. Don't underestimate the value of having a trusted confidante who is willing to listen, encourage you, and offer moral support during trying times. Sometimes the answer to your struggle may be right in front of you and all you needed to do was articulate the problem to see it. If you are feeling like giving up, your confidante can help you relax, reset, and get back on track. Unlike a peer mentor, a confidante is not necessarily a resource for solutions to problems, but a person to whom you can turn for emotional support.

The sixth type is the self-help mentor. This mentor is not a person, but a practically limitless collection of resources, including books, guides, articles, videos, blogs and technology with information and tools that can help you grow both personally and professionally. While not a substitute for an "external" mentor, self-help is available at all times on your phone, computer, and other smart technology, and is a viable substitute if a human mentor is unavailable for any reason, including financial limitations. Knowledge is power, especially meaningful, accurate and relevant knowledge acquired through your own resources. Self-help is most effectively used in conjunction with other types of mentors. Your commitment to chasing your dreams through self-help, particularly in light of, or despite, other challenges, may enhance your prospects of establishing an external relationship.

The seventh and final mentoring style is the inner mentor. This is a simple concept, yet difficult to use effectively. According to the Ohio State University research on the importance of mentors, the process of mentoring yourself takes "concentration, self-reflection, and the ability to trust your own instincts" (Metros and Yang). This is a sophisticated and mature process of objectively analyzing yourself - your experiences, your conduct, your goals, your interests, and your intentions. You must then be able to separate the good from the bad, and learn the right lessons from both. This requires intuition, intelligence, a developed moral compass, and an ability to be harsh, yet fair, to yourself. Not an easy task, yet the rewards from successful inner mentoring can be quite profound. As you experiment with this process, opening up to an external mentor or confidante would be an excellent way to assess how successful you are at objectively self-critiquing. While the self-mentor is an outward search for information, the inner mentor is an inward search for understanding, awareness and enlightenment.

It can be difficult to find a mentor. It is even harder to find the perfect mentor who has the time and resources to give you the guidance you need. As with so many needs and relationships, the challenges inherent in finding a mentor are now addressed on the Internet. Mike Garska, founder of FindAMentor.com, created the site that attempts to match you with mentors in your industry or field of interest for free!

A mentoring relationship should be mutually beneficial. The mentee gains the insight and wisdom of someone who has "been there." The mentor receives the satisfaction of perpetuating his or her knowledge, to both further their area of interest in general and guide a newcomer in particular. I suggest you write down the names of at least three people whom you would like to have as mentors, regardless of whether you know them or how crazy it would seem for you to even be able to make contact with them. If you already know them personally, reach out to them and offer to buy them a cup of coffee or take them out to lunch. In my experience, the best way to start the conversation is by asking your potential mentor "what is your story?" So many people have incredible stories to tell and are never provided an opportunity to tell them. Respectfully, professionally, and appropriately expressing your interest indicates to your potential mentor that you value his or her knowledge and experience and are willing to listen. Share your own story, but only to the extent appropriate and that they seem interested. Ideally, a potential mentor would come away from an initial meeting with an understanding that you are serious about your dream, that you have worked hard to gain insight into your area of interest, and that you would listen to and follow their advice.

Not every mentor is somebody with whom you will have a personal relationship, or even meet face to face. You can gain knowledge and motivation from people you don't know, without ever meeting them. Days after I officially registered Gothard Enterprises as an LLC, I happened across Jason Nazar's "The 21 Golden Rules of Entrepreneurship" video. His perspective on being an entrepreneur provided a different level of inspiration and confidence that I needed at the perfect time. One of the most powerful lessons Nazar taught was that there was nothing distinguishable between himself and anybody else. A prominent and successful businessman, he has accomplished a lot in his life, yet he claims that anybody can do what he has done with the right attitude and work ethic. We have never, and may never, meet in person, yet he has been an enormously impactful mentor to me.

Recently, I read "Good to Great" by Jim Collins. In this book, Collins outlines exactly what a company must do to achieve greatness. He defines leadership qualities needed for greatness, and coined the phrase "first who, then what," a profound concept that puts more emphasis on the people trying to achieve the goal than the goal itself. Collins teaches to confront and overcome the brutal facts with consistent, disciplined effort. With this knowledge, and that provided by Dr. Dweck about mindsets, I have a much clearer vision of how to successfully run my company and accomplish my goals in life.

LET'S SUMMARIZE!

1. Start pursuing your dreams now; it's never too early or too late.
2. Develop a plan.
3. Define and refine your dream.
4. Find passion for your journey.
5. Maintain a strong work ethic and persevere throughout.
6. Work towards the right mindset and be confident.
7. Figure out your capital needs and raise what you can.
8. Find a mentor.

I am not claiming to have achieved anything spectacular in my life, but I am proud to say that I'm trying. I wake up everyday thinking about how to reach my next goal, and that gives meaning to my life. I had a dream of starting a company. At 20 years old, I accomplished that. Now, at 21 years of age, my dream is to build my company into a great one and to continue writing. Hopefully my story can be of some use to you in pursuing your dreams.

One final suggestion is to enjoy the journey. Not every endeavor is successful, and not every path ends up where you think it will. You might even end up accomplishing a completely different goal than you set out to, which could be far more rewarding than what you set out to accomplish. Pursue your journey with passion. What you may gain along the way, and learn about the world and about yourself, may be worth more to you than the original goal.

I will conclude with anecdotes of three very different, but all incredibly successful people. I hope that their stories are as inspirational to you as they are to me.

MARTIN VILLENUEVE

History has proven that there will always be amazing people who change the world. Some, like director, producer, and actor Martin Villeneuve, don't even realize that they are doing so. In his TEDx talk, Villeneuve claims he "made a film that was impossible to make, but [he] didn't know it was impossible, and that's how [he] was able to do it." His science fiction film, "Mars et Avril," is set in Montreal about 50 years in the future. To bring his vision to life, he needed about $23 million, an arsenal of visual effects, an incredible cast, and a vision of a futuristic Quebec that would resonate with the public. Through determination, an entrepreneurial spirit, and a lot of hard work, he made his film with a budget of $2.3 million. What was his secret? First and foremost was time - he spent seven years working on his film, perfecting every single shot from start to finish. Next was the support of those around him. He attributes much of his success to those that worked with him on the film. Collectively, they had a positive mindset, turning every problem into an opportunity. For example, when one of their starring actors was too busy to be able to stay on set as long as needed, Villeneuve, jokingly said they should make the actor into a hologram. They took action, filming hundreds (maybe even thousands) of scenes from six different angles, all upwards from the shoulder. On set, another man mimed what the original actor was supposed to be doing. Villeneuve digitally replaced the mime's head with the head of the original actor. Villeneuve said that if you treat problems as opportunities, "life will start to dance with you in the most amazing way." Since the Quebec premiere of "Mars et Avril" in 2012, it has been shown at more than 20 international film festivals.

ROALD AMUNDSEN

Some, like explorer Roald Amundsen, work their whole lives to change the world. Amundsen made a decision at an early age that he would never stop exploring the wilderness. At 25 years old, he was first mate on the Belgian Antarctic Expedition (1897-99) under Baron Adrein de Gerlache, an officer in the Belgian Royal Navy. Sailing in the RV Belgica, the crew became the first expedition to spend an entire winter in Antarctica. Amundsen was an observant man, and learned from the veterans of the expedition. For example, when the crew faced scurvy on their voyage, the ship's doctor went hunting, theorizing that fresh meat from most animals contains enough vitamin C to fight and even prevent the disease. In 1903, Amundsen was the first to explore Canada's Northwest Passage between the Atlantic and Pacific Oceans.

On this journey, he learned fundamental Arctic survival tactics from native Inuits. On June 3, 1910, Amundsen set off on his greatest challenge, the South Pole Expedition. By January 14, 1911, the crew had established the base camp Framheim at the Great Ice Barrier in Antarctica. He learned from the Inuits to use sled dogs, rather than heavier horses, to traverse the landscape and to use animal skins, rather than heavy wool clothing, to stay warm in the frigid Arctic. Despite their precautions, the expedition's first trek from base camp to the pole, September 8, 1911, was a failure due to extreme temperatures and quarreling within the group. By October 19, 1911, the team was ready to try again, this time discovering a path on the Axel Heiberg Glacier. On December 14, 1911, Roald Amundsen became the first man to successfully reach the South Pole. The great explorer has become a legend. In his book, The South Pole, Amundsen writes "victory awaits him who has everything in order—luck, people call it. Defeat is certain for him who has neglected to take the necessary precautions in time; this is called bad luck."

SOL GOTHARD

Like Villeneuve, the director and producer who achieved notoriety within the film industry, and Amundsen, the legendary explorer who conquered the South Pole, my grandfather has proven to be an incredible and inspiring figure. Born in 1930 to an abusive father and a destitute household, he spent a lot of his youth with social workers. He worked multiple jobs and put himself through high school and college before being drafted into the army in 1953. After an honorary discharge in 1955, he enrolled in and paid his way through the Graduate School of Social Work at Case Western Reserve University in Cleveland. His inspiration and motivation to be the first in his family to succeed in college and graduate school came from his mentors, the social workers who were so influential in his younger days. They created a passion in him to help others, just as they had helped him. After graduating with a Masters in Social Work, my grandfather married and moved to New Orleans to start a life with my grandmother. He worked as a probation officer in the Jefferson Parish Juvenile Court and learned that the ultimate decision makers in creating and implementing meaningful programs to help those caught in the justice system were the judges, specifically juvenile court judges. Unfortunately, one needed to be a lawyer to qualify to run for judicial office. At that time, he was working full time as a probation officer, earning just enough to support his growing family. But he had a dream, he had a passion, and he would not be deterred. So, he enrolled in night classes at the Loyola University Law School in 1958. After graduating in 1962 and practicing law for ten years, he ran for Judge of the Jefferson Parish Juvenile Court in 1972. "Never in the world did I expect to win," my grandfather told me, "I was a poor, Jewish social worker from New York." He had no political connections or support, and not a great deal of money to finance a campaign. So he campaigned the old school way – door-to-door solicitation, and personal phone calls - using his slogan Not Just Another Lawyer to distinguish himself from a crowded slate of candidates. Against all odds, and due to his perseverance, he became the second Judge in the history of the Jefferson Parish Juvenile Court after winning with 75% of the popular vote. After sitting on the Juvenile Court bench for 14 years, he was elected Judge of the Louisiana Fifth

Circuit Court of Appeal in 1986, the second highest court in the State of Louisiana, where he served until his retirement in 2005.

His passion was to help others, particularly troubled youth, just as he had been helped. He made that his life's goal, far surpassing his initial aspirations to be a social worker. As a judge, he was able to create programs to assist juveniles throughout the juvenile justice system in innovative and effective ways. Through this work he became a nationally recognized expert in this field, and was asked to teach graduate social work students at Tulane University, where he reached the rank of Full Adjunct Professor of Social Work and Law. He has spoken at numerous regional, national, and international conferences all across the United States, not just on juvenile issues, but on diverse topics in the fields of social work, psychology, psychiatry, law, pediatrics, and law enforcement. His interests ranged beyond juvenile issues to concern for abused animals, American veterans, and battered women. The common theme was always his passion and concern for the defense of the less fortunate, less powerful, and more vulnerable members of our society. He has authored hundreds of articles that have been published in numerous journals, including the Journal of the National Council of Juvenile and Family Court Judges, Journal of the National Organization of Forensic Social Work, and Journal of The American Professional Society on the Abuse of Children. Of his humble beginnings, my grandfather has always said, "the negatives did not define my life. The positives did." Throughout his long and distinguished career, he brought positive change to thousands of people. My grandfather's story is proof that anybody can accomplish his or her goals, regardless of where you start. I hope you can find motivation through his struggles. Like he always says, "you must have a goal. Throughout life, I am firmly convinced you have to be aiming for something all the time."

The purpose of this book is to help you chase your dreams. In your life, I challenge you to wake up every single day and try to take the next step towards your goal. If you do, you will find that your once impossible dreams can turn into incredible accomplishments. And who knows, you might even have a little fun along the way.

AUTHOR'S NOTE

Thank you so much for reading my first book! I have worked extremely hard on this book, but publishing it isn't the end. I want to get your feedback on how I can improve as a writer and entrepreneur, so please leave me a review on Amazon.

Bibliography

"2013 Champions." Peoples Health Champions: Meet the
    Champions. Peoples Health, n.d. Web. 27 July 2015.
    <http://www.peopleshealth.com/champions/pages/meet
    _the_champions/2013-Sol_Gothard.shtml>.
"American Time Use Survey Summary." U.S. Bureau of
    Labor Statistics. U.S. Bureau of Labor Statistics, 24 June
    2015. Web. 12 July 2015.
    <http://www.bls.gov/news.release/atus.nr0.htm/>.
Coleman, Ben. "NOFSW Honors Sol Gothard with
    Achievement Award." National Organization of Forensic
    Social Work. NOSFW, n.d. Web. 30 July 2015.
    <http://nofsw.org/?p=143>.
Cooper, Bell Beth. "A Brilliant Story of Chasing Your
    Dreams When People Say It's Impossible, by @attendly."
    Attendly. Attendly, n.d. Web. 12 July 2015.
    <http://www.attendly.com/a-brilliant-story-of-chasing-
    your-dreams-when-people-say-its-impossible/>.
"Court Role and Structure." United States Courts.
    Administrative Office of the U.S. Courts, n.d. Web. 30
    July 2015. <http://www.uscourts.gov/about-federal-
    courts/court-role-and-structure>.
Heppner, Jake. "30 Surprising Facts About How We Actually
    Spend Our Time." Distractify. N.p., n.d. Web. 12 July
    2015. <https://www.distractify.com/astounding-facts-
    about-how-we-actually-spend-our-time-
    1197818577.html>.
Jones, Jeromie. "Obstacles to Achieving Your Dreams."
    Jeromiejones.com. N.p., 07 Oct. 2013. Web. 12 July 2015.
    <http://jeromiejones.com/2013/10/07/the-biggest-

obstacle-to-achieving-your-dreams/>.

"Judge Sol Gothard." Judge Sol Gothard. Center for Judicial Excellence, 12 Feb. 2014. Web. 30 July 2015. <http://www.centerforjudicialexcellence.org/multimedia/ kids-of-divorce-speak-out/judge-sol-gothard/>.

Manfred, Tony. "Mark Cuban Explains The Most Important Part Of Having A Strong Work Ethic." Business Insider. Business Insider, Inc, 11 Nov. 2014. Web. 12 July 2015. <http://www.businessinsider.com/mark-cuban-on-dirk-nowitzkis-work-ethic-2014-11>.

Metros, Susan E., and Catherine Yang. "Chapter 5: The Importance of Mentors." Chapter 5: The Importance of Mentors. EDUCAUSE, n.d. Web. 07 July 2015. <http://www.educause.edu/research-publications/books/cultivating-careers-professional-development-campus-it/chapter-5-importance-mentors>.

Parrish, Shane. "The Two Mindsets and the Power of Believing That You Can Improve." Time. Time, n.d. Web. 12 July 2015. <http://time.com/3765563/carol-dweck-two-mindsets/>.

"Roald Amundsen." PBS. PBS, n.d. Web. 12 July 2015. <http://www.pbs.org/wgbh/amex/ice/peopleevents/pa ndeAMEX87.html>.

"Roald Amundsen." Wikipedia. Wikimedia Foundation, n.d. Web. 12 July 2015. <https://en.wikipedia.org/wiki/Roald_Amundsen#cite_n ote-Mifflin-6>.

Wells, Jonathan. "What It Takes to Accomplish Your Goals and Dreams." Advanced Life Skills. N.p., n.d. Web. 12 July 2015. <http%3A%2F%2Fadvancedlifeskills.com%2Fblog%2Fw hat-it-takes-to-accomplish-your-dreams%2F>.

CEO at 20: A Little Book for Big Dreams